A SENSELESS TEEN MURDER & THE HARDKNOCK LIFE

SAN QUENTIN & LA STATE PRISON

EAST OAKLAND TIMES, LLC

EAST OAKLAND

"Sometimes you struggle so hard to feed your family one way, you forget to feed them the other way, with spiritual nourishment. Everybody needs that."

— JAMES BROWN, AMERICAN MUSICIAN

MY CRIME SERIES - BOOK EIGHT

A SENSELESS TEEN MURDER & THE HARDKNOCK LIFE

Welcome to San Quentin State Prison! Come and meet your new "cellies." Their names are Daniel Davidson and Curtis Frazier and they have a story to tell about the origins and the exercise of a "killer mentality."

The books of the My Crime series are neither meant to justify nor condemn the inmates on whom they are written. Rather, the books of the My Crime series propose to candidly communicate the upbringing, life experience, and motivations of the incarcerated.

The My Crime series puts you as the judge. Your judgment will not simply be about the individual on whom a book is written, but your judgment will weigh the life circumstances that shaped his or her criminal disposition. The My Crime series takes the unknown inmate and presents his or her life for public evaluation.

Each book in the My Crime series is written on an inmate, by an inmate. Each book will progress from the subject's childhood up through the commitment offense that brought about the subject's current felony incarceration. Each book, therefore, will offer a window into the subject's criminality as dictated to and written by a fellow inmate.

The My Crime series books are intended to fit into the present day dialog on crime and punishment. As citizens of California's democracy within the United States, the understanding we each have of right and wrong is the most essential knowledge we can use in taking political positions. Ideally, the justice issued by state, county, city, and, potentially, regional lawmakers, as interpreted by the courts, is a justice that agrees with citizens. If citizens agree with the justice being issued by an elected government, citizens will tend to promote that justice as truth for the times.

The My Crime series intends to bring Californias together in an understanding of the life experience of California felons. Through the My Crime series, you gain the opportunity to sit and listen to the unknown felon and learn, as if you were on the bottom bunk, about your neighbor and what brought him or her to getting locked up.

Thank you for purchasing the eighth book in the My Crime series.

PLEASE REVIEW *A SENSELESS TEEN MURDER & THE HARDKNOCK LIFE* ON AMAZON!

I welcome you to visit the webpage dedicated to this series to find more crime biographies and audio interviews: crimebios.com

Finally, read the last page of this book for a broad understanding of the philosophy of the producer of the My Crime series, the East Oakland Times, LLC.

Tio MacDonald
Founder & Chief Editor

A SENSELESS TEEN MURDER

1

INTRODUCTION

Prison is like a nightmare that keeps repeating itself; it's a horror story on a loop. Prison is the place where I am becoming a man. Prison is where I have grown up and learned how to connect the dots of my childhood anger to the worst deed one could ever commit, all before the age of eighteen.

It wasn't until I stopped blaming others and took responsibility for my actions that I began to accept my fate and do some real and honest introspection. While I am still a work in progress, after four years of incarceration, I have concluded that I am in prison for the bad decisions I made, and no matter who influenced those decisions, I was the one who made the choice that landed me in the big house. In-depth and continuous self-reflection helped me recognize how a sixteen-year-old me, Daniel Davidson, could end up sentenced to 26 years to life for first-degree murder.

DANIEL'S FAMILY

L ife for me and my six siblings began in a small city in Southern California called Victorville. I was raised in Victorville by my mom and my stepfather. My mom, Ana, a short, nice-looking white woman, is the greatest mother in the world. She is loving, affectionate, and very protective of her children, even into adulthood. She is the model of hard-working and sound decision making. It was right decision making that led her to divorce my biological father, Gerald, when I was about three-years-old, and marry Ismael, a short, buff Mexican man with a beer belly and a good heart. My biological father was in and out of jail for one thing or another. He wasn't a good provider or role model. When I look in the mirror today, I can't help but wonder if Gerald's affinity for prison was somehow a forerunner of my own fate - a fate that skipped incarceration on the installment plan and cashed in with a mega-winner. In contrast, my stepfather Ismael loved us as if we were his own. He is a family man, attentive, caring, and responsible.

We were a close-knit family. Ana and Ismael did their best to provide for us. They had seven riotous boys under the roof. Mom and Ismael worked tirelessly to put food on the table. We struggled financially. At first, I was too young to understand what that meant to be embarrassed about it. At one point, we relied on public assistance. My early years lacked any luxuries. Our clothes and shoes had to last throughout the school year. It wasn't until I got older that I realized just how much my parents sacrificed for us.

A large part of the reason for the financial struggle is that my parents resolved to provide the best education for us that money could buy by sending us to private school. Initially, private school was fun. I had lots of friends and I felt comfortable. Eventually, I took for granted the new books, the clean classrooms, and the clean facilities that private schools offer.

Financial troubles didn't stop us from having fun. I remember many occurrences where fun was the staple of life, and that was enough for me. Kids live for fun, at least I did, and I had plenty of it. I recall many nights when we enjoyed pizza together. We'd talk and play with each other, joke around, and just have a ball. Those were the good times, full of fun, but empty pockets. For the most part, I remember being a happy kid. I had all that mattered, love safety, food, and fun. Life was as simple as that back then.

Of all of my brothers, I was closest to Chris, who was a year my senior. I looked up to Chris, and by age 11, I was his constant shadow. When he hung out at parties, I was right there with him. I'd watch Chris at these parties, and take notes, learning how to be cool and slick. He didn't always invite me, but I was still right there, next to him, behind him, somewhere near. When he smoked weed, I took a tote, too. It was my first time and I liked it! Chris was the one that guided and I willingly made the choices to follow.

Whoever picked a fight with me, had to fight Chris as well. And whoever he fought, had to fight me. Sometimes we fought each other. Those were lesson sessions for me. I learned defensive and offensive fighting with Chris because even when we were mad, I knew he wasn't trying to hurt me. There were never any winners in our fights against each other. It was like best friends fighting each other.

I remember my parents threw a party one night. That was the night the lights went out during the festivities and someone stole the DJ's laptop during the confusion. A fight broke out in the dark and the house was trashed. That was the same night I saw Chris sneak into the house, hide some beers in his jacket, and deliver them to us as we waited outside. I thought Chris had the biggest balls in the world for that. When Chris finally outgrew me and wanted to venture out on his own, with kids his age, it was those fights we had before that gave me the confidence to survive the future fights that were inevitably my fate. It was that rough training that helped me get through school and later my neighborhood, then Youth Authority, and now prison. When Chris left me for his friends, I was mad at first, but I thought it was also ballsy. I wanted to be like him so much; I accepted that if Chris did it, it was right. There must've been something I could learn from it. What I learned from Chris' split from me was how to be confident and independent.

My mixed-lineage gives me a unique look. I am often told that I have bright eyes, *ojos claros*, as my Mexican side would say. I am often told that I have a warm smile. My temper stems, I imagine, from my paternal Native American side. Anger became the side-kick that replaced Chris as I got older and more defiant. It didn't take much to set me off. It seems, the closer I got to anger, the further I got from my white side, a part of me I never really embraced. Likely because, other than my wonderful mother, everyone around me was either Mexican or black.

In my mind, my mom wasn't white; she was just my mom. When we hung out together in public, she was just "mom." When she cheered me on in the stands as I played football, baseball, or water polo, mom was just mom, a beautiful human being, a person I will forever love and admire. It was the coolest feeling in the world to have my mom there supporting me and cheering me on. My mom is the one person I know cheers me on with happiness and pride when I do good, so it motivated me in sports to have her there, jumping and hollering in the stands.

Again, the early years were tough financially. It wasn't until later that my mom finished her schooling and became a successful real estate agent, and Ismael graduated from welding school that things truly improved for us. Getting hard-earned money delivered us from the poverty that had strangled us so deftly when I was growing up.

ELEMENTARY SCHOOL

E lementary school taught me three things: (1) I wasn't interested in school, (2) kids can be cruel, and (3) violence is the best way to tame mean kids.

The teasing started when the other kids noticed that I couldn't stand up straight. I was born with scoliosis, an abnormal curvature of the spine. Once that secret was out, school wasn't so fun anymore. Fun turned to anger and hate in a flash. I hated the way the other kids treated me. I hadn't done anything to them. They made me feel less than and disconnected from them. I felt betrayed because, up until then, everything was fine, even great. I was "normal" and they were friendly. Then, just like that! Everything changed! My violent responses put me at odds with the teachers, which led to issues with authority that I still deal with today. There's only one authority figure in my life that I can comfortably submit to, my mom.

Fighting the other kids became a routine for a while until they realized that my anger fueled my wins and they needed to back off. I was never a bully, though. I didn't fight because I liked it. I fought to protect myself. I fought to make them stop teasing and bullying me. I fought to protect others from the same treatment, but I never instigated a fight. I didn't like fighting for the sake of fighting, but I did like it when they respected me or even feared me. Their fear of me became a point of security for me. The reward of my violent behavior was respect from the other kids. I couldn't stand straight, but I had a mean right. Fighting was the medium I used to "play" with the other kids. Fighting gave me a chance to prove that despite the curvature in my spine, I could perform just as good as the best of them.

Elementary was a mix of fun, triumphs, violence, and failures. Lectures from the principal escalated to suspensions and suspensions led to my expulsion. I ended up getting suspended at least eight times. I mostly was suspended for fighting other kids and cursing out teachers. I was expelled for carrying a gun to school, though it was only a BB gun (A girl saw the toy in my backpack and told a teacher. I felt betrayed.)

This was the period in my life when I first experienced depression. I was only ten-years-old, but the rejection of the other kids and their abrupt turn from me was a turning point in my life. The experience showed me just how cruel people could be. The lesson was to dish out what I received, but ten times worse. I always had to get the last laugh. As the years went by, and my reputation sustained my respect, I could relax. When I got expelled from school, then I had to show my ugly side again. It became a cycle until I was a teen.

As much as I respect and appreciate Ismael, even he got the bad side of my rebellion when I was a teen. Whether it was Ismael hitting Chris or Ismael trying to discipline me with a ruler or an extension cord, I just wasn't having it. My violent response to Ismael's attempt to punish me was message enough that I was too grown to submit, though I was just a teen. It was a very frustrating time for me.

The teasing, the fighting, and the principal's office were enough of a distraction to keep my grades low, along with my academic confidence. My preference was toward having fun, not homework and studies. I hated homework. My head simply was not into concentrating. I was preoccupied with the here and now and had little interest in preparing for the future. I was a mediocre student then and remain one today. My mediocrity was not and is not embarrassing; it isn't that I can't do the work, I just have no interest. Of course, my mom was disappointed with my grades. Even her disappointment wasn't enough to motivate me to do better. My best grades came in physical education, with mostly B grades. These grade achievements did not excite me because I simply had no interest in school. They just showed me that I could do it if I wanted to.

I loved sports then and I love sports now. I am happiest when I play sports, even in prison. It all started when I was five. I played basketball. I used to feel important when everyone was looking at me hold the bat and swing. I didn't do anything special with it until three years later when I hit a home run. That felt great, like I was a king. It was the same feeling when I hit a basket while playing hoops, or kicked the ball past a goalie. Those were the days. In prison, I am respected even more because I can play with skill despite my scoliosis. If only my elementary peers would have seen it that way.

APPLE VALLEY, CALIFORNIA

We moved from Victorville to Apple Valley, just a hop, skip, and a jump from my city of birth. Apple Valley reflects most of my memories of life and experience. Apple Valley's racial make-up was mixed with primarily blacks and Hispanics. There were a few gangs and Apple Valley's gangs had their violent rivals. I never joined a gang, though I was invited. With gangs came robberies, beatings, and shootings. I wasn't interested in all of that. I just wanted to have fun, make friends, be cool. Illegal drugs and prostitution were also part of the Apple Valley scene.

Alcohol and drugs were as easy for me to get as candy. All I had to do was ask one of the older guys in the neighborhood. As long as I had the money, it was all right. Sometimes I got dope for free! My drinks of choice were the hard stuff, Bacardi and Patron. The good stuff. Weapons were just as easy to find. Over the years, I was able to get an assortment of guns for cheap. The most I paid for any gun was $100. I had a .32 caliber, a 9-millimeter, and a couple of shotguns. Ironically, it wasn't my use of one of these numerous guns that led to my incarceration. Weapons were so normal to me that I never worried about the police stopping me while armed.

A police presence was another part of our neighborhood, but in another form. Apple Valley is like a hick town, small with an even smaller budget. Paid security roamed the streets, stopping people, searching people, harassing people. They mainly focused on blacks and conducted their job in offensive ways. They were jerks to the fullest and proof to me that it isn't just white cops who can be racists, but people with power. The security detail was primarily Hispanic.

It got personal for me when they started coming to my house and tearing up our backyard or harassing us on our property. They kept saying the neighbors were complaining that we were making too much noise, but that was a lie. We were good with our neighbors; our neighbors would have simply talked to us if there was a problem. Looking back, they had no right to go on our property. That said, police visits to my house were the extent of it. I don't recall ever being harassed on the streets like my other friends.

DANIEL AS A KID

L ike most kids, I just wanted to fit in with the others in my neighborhood. I wanted the respect of the other boys and I wanted the girls to love me. Chris showed me early on what it meant to have balls and what it felt like to have courage. It felt empowering, even if my measure for courage was warped. To say I was peer pressured would be a mischaracterization. I was a willing participant in every illegal activity I was part of, for curiosity's sake, for respect, for fun. At most, I was egged on, encouraged beyond my reluctance to move past any hesitation: "It's cool." "It'll be alright." "Just do it, man," were some of the reassurances I'd receive from others. They simply made me want to do it more. I take full responsibility for my actions. I own all of my decisions, even up to the murder that was regrettably to come.

I would say that I went to the neighborhood with balls and courage. Courage gave me the balls to brazenly steal candy bars out of the local stores. Courage gave me the balls to slash the neighbors' tires and play ding-dong ditch, our style of fun. Courage gave me the balls to lay shotgun shells on train tracks and watch them light up while ducking and dodging the spray of pellets. It might as well have been a game of group Russian roulette. I guess you could say we, my friends and I, survived ourselves. To us, our mischief was just the normal activity of raucous teens. We didn't think about the consequences; we didn't fully understand consequences and thus had little concern for consequences, other than not getting caught.

My dogs and weed were my escape mechanisms. I owned mostly pit bulls. I didn't train them to be aggressive or anything like that. I just liked that breed. They looked cool. Even so, Olive was my favorite of all the dogs. Olive was a sweet black lab. I loved to walk her and play with her. She was the most loving and affectionate of all my dogs.

I began using drugs around eleven years old. Weed made me feel like I was a king. I liked the feeling, the light-headedness, the way it slowed things down as if everything was in a crisp slow motion. It was something fun to do with my neighborhood friends. These were the guys who accepted me, respected me, and treated me like their own. There was nothing to prove. I didn't have to be macho, just cool.

I remember Ismael finding my stash a few times, just weed, or a bong, nothing serious. Of course, he was furious the first time he found pot in the house. Ismael was furious each time he found drugs in the house, but my brother Chris and I just kind of got used to it, numbed ourselves, and tried to be more careful. Ismael really had no effect in guiding us, though he tried. Even his threats to boot us out of the house fell on deaf ears. There's no way mom would go for that, he knew that and so did we.

Eleven was the age I had my first lay. I never had problems with girls. I wasn't shy and they accepted me like the rest of the neighborhood kids. Millie was my first sexual experience. Millie and I were just messing around, kissing, and feeling each other up; one thing led to another. I let her lead the way. Clothes started coming off; she was feeling it, and the next thing I knew, we were at it. We did it at my house, in my room. We did it behind the school, where the buildings blocked prying eyes and gave us privacy. We did it wherever we felt we could get away with it. It was the best feeling in the world. It was awesome! We never got caught. I had lots of girlfriends after that, but there was only one girl that stole my heart and would become the star of my heart.

6

HIGH SCHOOL

High school was the best experience as far as school went. I got along with the other kids, they respected me and it was a lot of fun. High school was when I began to excel in sports. I played baseball, basketball, and soccer. I played hard and the team rewarded me with praise and worth. My mom was also there in the stands, faithfully cheering me on. It was the best feeling in the world to be normal, to be loved, and to be good at something that I liked to do.

All of that was on the field. The classroom was another story as I struggled to make my grades and meet the approval of my teachers. I didn't get in trouble as much because the kids treated me fine. I still rebelled against the teachers because they pressured me to do things I didn't want to do or things I wasn't good at. That's how I saw it.

I ditched class a lot, hanging out and getting high. To pay for the dope, I hustled weed. I'd buy a score from the older homeboys in the neighborhood and flip it for a modest profit. I wasn't trying to get rich, just keep what I had going without hitting up my parents. Coke was the real drain on my pockets. I got introduced to coke through this older girl named Tiffany. We were partying, smoking weed at her parents' house. Tiffany pulled out some coke and was like, "Party with this!" I had never seen cocaine before, but I was curious; I wanted to try it for her. I liked her. I looked up to her and wanted to impress her. It was a much different high than weed. For me, weed made me relaxed. I just wanted to kickback. Coke made me hyper. It made me want to go.

I ended up doing coke for about a year with Tiffany. We partied with it. I don't know what it was about me that attracted Tiffany, but I wanted to be with her. She was mature, smart, and edgy. She knew about life. Tiffany taught me more about the drug life, about powder and crack cocaine, about smack. She hooked me up with other dealers and new ways to hustle. She taught me new sex positions, which was fun. We had sex a lot and that was nice too. But then I found out that she was seeing other dudes and I wasn't feelin' that. I was hurt and felt betrayed by her. I thought we had something special going on. Tiffany was nothing but a whore; that's how she could afford coke and not work or hustle for it. So I ended up doing coke for about a year. In the end, I didn't like the hyper feeling and my reason to stick with that type of high disappeared with Tiffany. I am a laid back person; weed fits my personality better. Plus, coke was expensive. I was paying up to four times more for coke than for weed, which meant I had to hustle hard for less high. It just wasn't worth it.

Another thing that just wasn't worth it was trying to find girls online. There was this girl at our school named Wendy. I really liked her. Wendy was cute, short, had a bubbly personality, and was laid back like me. One day I was messing around online and found her profile. I was high and just having fun. So I hit her up and she responded. Things were going nice; we were having a good conversation. When she told me to meet her at the park the next day, I got excited. I like older girls.

Little did I know the whole thing was a setup. It was Wendy's picture online. It was Wendy's account, but it was Wendy's boyfriend I had been flirting with. I went to the park alone, with no gun, or knife because I thought it was just a simple date with Wendy. I was confronted by Wendy's boyfriend and his three partners. Her boyfriend wanted to fight me while his homeboys recorded it. But that was bull; they were going to jump me. I know how the game goes. The minute I got the advantage, they'd be on me like a fly on shit. I remember my heart beating desperately, and my mouth was so dry I could hardly talk. I thought I was going to die that night. I told Wendy's boyfriend that I didn't know Wendy had a boyfriend, which was true. I told him that I meant no disrespect. Somehow, I talked my way out of it and got out of there. But if I had had my gun, I definitely would have taken him on and even shot him and his homeboys if I had to. The joint that I had after that incident was the best joint I ever had! I don't think I ever needed a dose of calm more than I did that night!

7

DANIEL'S GIRLFRIEND

W hile I didn't know that Wendy had a boyfriend, I did know that Ashley was my girl and that she had always been faithful to me. Ashley and I met when we were young. Some friends hooked us up. I thought she was the most beautiful girl on earth. She wore glasses; she was two years older and kind of nerdy, which I liked. Ashley also had dark brown hair, a cute set of chipmunk cheeks, with a thick body type and a five-foot one-inch frame – a huge five inches shorter than me! We were made for each other. We basically grew up together.

I met her during middle school and we quickly became the best of friends. We did everything together. And I was proud that almost everything we did together was her first. I was her first real boyfriend. I was the first to lay with her. I introduced her to weed. And I didn't feel bad about hooking her up with weed because God made it. I felt like if God made it, it can't be bad. I still feel that way, at least right now. But I'm open to change. Anyway, Ashley is my best friend; she is the best thing that ever happened to me. Ashley is the first person, outside of family, that truly understands me.

We hung out at school, at my house or her house, and in the neighborhood, mostly in the park. We joked and laughed. We talked about the here and now and dreamed of the future. It was always a good time with Ashley, never any arguments or conflict. Looking back, Ashley was the only one that made me truly happy.

Unfortunately, I took a lot for granted then, especially Ashley. I neglected her, talking with other girls, partying with other girls, and screwing other girls, yet, Ashley hung with me. The other girls meant nothing to me, really. I thought I wanted more, not realizing that Ashley was all I needed. I thought I was having fun, but in retrospect, I don't even remember half the girls I was with. What's worse is that I used to get jealous, big time, if I saw her talking to other guys. My chest would get red hot and my breathing would increase. I hated it when she was with other guys. And she hated it when I was with other girls, but she hated in silence, while I expressed my displeasure in not so loving ways.

Back then, I had no idea what love, healthy love, was. I didn't know how to express it. The reason for that is that I never stopped to think about it. I was too busy thinking about myself, instead of stopping to recall how my own family cared for me. My family was the perfect model, had I paid attention. Even Ismael's love for me was about as good as it gets. He always treated me like his own. I took it all for granted. I had a lot of growing up to do.

It was as if Ashley knew I was immature and was silently, patiently waiting on the mature Danny to emerge. While Ashley was a positive influence on my life, I had a corrupting and destructive impact on her life. Again, I was her first sexual partner, the first person to introduce her to drugs, and the person to break her heart over and over again.

Despite all of the negativity I brought to her life, Ashley stuck with me unconditionally, loving me as patiently and unconditionally as my mom. I recognize Ashley's love for me now. I've nearly lost her twice. The thought of losing Ashley was as devastating as my arrest for murder.

I was in the California Youth Authority (Y.A.) when we suffered our first break up. It had been a year and we were growing apart. Our phone calls were contentious, as we argued over the petty details of life. It was then that I thought I hated her. I was so mad at Ashley that I cussed out my mom. My mom was our liaison; she is the one who kept us together, encouraging us to talk and listen to one another. So we continued to talk and write. Back then, we were simply putting up with one another.

Eventually, I learned that Ashley had become pregnant by another guy out there. I never felt so helpless in my life. There was nothing I could do about it. I felt that my world had ended. It was then that I realized just how much Ashley meant to me. Ashley is irreplaceable. That is now clear to me. As time went on, we remained friends. Ashley convinced me that I still have value. I am beginning to see that now. The more I learn and accomplish, the more I see my worth and potential. Whatever potential I have is enhanced with Ashley at my side.

We grew up together and we are continuing to grow and mature. I have learned to value that. As it turns out, Ashley is the best friend I have ever had. Ashely is the person who has defined loyalty, true love, and respect to me. As individuals, neither of us have been perfect, we've made some awful decisions, but together we are the perfect couple. I believe nothing can prevail against us. We bring out the best in each other.

I guess that's why I feel so bad about how I dogged her. Ashley has always been there for me. While she was loyal to me, I was out messing around with any and every girl I could convince to give me attention. It was all about fun for me at that age. I just liked to have fun, so I didn't think about people's feelings or consequences or anything like that. Yet Ashley was the only girl that I took home that my mom accepted. And her entire family received me - her cousins, aunts, and everyone. They treated me as if I was part of the family. Ashley is the first girl that I can say I truly loved. I hope to walk down the aisle with Ashley one day. I would be the happiest man ever. I get emotional thinking about it. Other than my mom and Chris, Ashley is the only other person I feel a deep connection to.

Despite the way I treated Ashley, she always put me first. Other than my mom, no other girl has loved me as deeply and unconditionally. She is the best friend I had ever had. Unfortunately, I didn't realize that until after the damage had been done. When I got locked up for murder, I think that scared Ashely. She didn't know what to think. Still, she stuck with me while I was in juvie. My time there really put a strain on our relationship. To my surprise, it was her mom that came to my defense. Kathy still believes in me. In fact, Kathy is in denial about the whole thing. She doesn't believe I killed Marlo Williams. The only problem is that I did do it. I must accept responsibility as much as I am ashamed to do so. That's one of the first things I learned in prison, to take responsibility, to man up.

8

DEATHS IN THE FAMILY

Before I could experience the bliss of love, the drama of death, and more death, struck my family and me like a plague. I was just about to begin my teen years when the life of my precious maternal great aunt, Lydia, passed away. It was one of the sadder days of my life. Lydia was just as loving, affectionate, and caring as my mom. I felt connected to her and her love for me was authentic and unconditional. She was the rock that held the family together.

What I remember most about Lydia was the family outings at her house. We would visit her mainly on birthdays and holidays. Even Super Bowls were made that much more super at her home. It was always a family affair, which I loved. Lydia's house was huge, like a mansion. It had a swimming pool, fireplace, a huge back patio, and an impressive overhead canopy. Under the canopy was a volleyball net and we could remove the net to play soccer. There were fruit trees and a separate shed for the boat and car. It was always a good time.

Her death had a massive impact on me. The loss of Lydia came at the same time I was having issues with rebellion. I rebelled against Ismael as he attempted to impose his will on me. I rebelled against the teachers and other authority figures as they pressed and pressed. It was at a time in my young life that I was coming into my own, trying to figure out who I was, what I wanted to be. I wanted to assert my own will, not be ordered and directed by a father figure, teachers, or principals.

I remember crying on the porch at Lydia's house. I remember crying at the funeral with everyone else. It was so sad that I still remember how it felt. I could cry as I write this now. What made it worse was seeing my mom heartbroken. It was a horrible time for our family. I was struggling and our family was struggling. The family was in such financial distress. We were so desperate that we went to live at my defunct Aunt Lydia's house. I was excited because Aunt Lydia's home is where many of my fondest memories came to life. Jeremey, Lydia's husband, accepted us initially, but soon after he kicked us out for his new girlfriend. I couldn't believe that Jeremy would give us the boot. He traded family for some new girl he had just met. She wasn't even that hot! I felt betrayed by his rejection of us. That incident kind of locked in what a dog-eat-dog world we live in and created another character defect for me: the fear of rejection. I couldn't trust friends or family it turned out.

My mom was just about finished with her schooling to be a real estate agent and Ismael had almost completed his training as a welder, so it didn't take long for us to get back on our feet and even prosper. Our rebound from the humiliation of Jeremy's rejection was pretty remarkable. Everything was going great. We were beyond our financial worries, but the loss and pain would continue.

Sometime later, my grandpa, Benny, died. Benny was Ismael's father. Even though I didn't know him that well, I was devastated. I saw how Ismael was affected and I felt terrible for him. I had met Benny a few times and he was cool. How I knew him best was by the stories Ismael's side told of him. They said he was a good man, a hard-working man, and a generous man. What was more impactful was that Benny's death followed Lydia's death. We barely had time to heal – if that is even possible – before we were all mourning again. The already somber mood sunk deeper into sorrow.

As if that wasn't enough, my Grandma, Estela, died right after that. Her death made me think about life and what it meant. What is the purpose? I'm still working on that. Estela was old school. She was kind and warm but drew the line. I can't say we were close, because I wasn't exposed to her much, but the few times I saw her, she was a nice older lady and was always kind to me. Still, sorrow is contagious and Estella's death had a profound effect on the rest of the family. It was as if we had a continuous dark cloud hovering over and within our house. Our financial struggles were contained and even conquered, but death was out of anyone's control and that was something I came to realize real quick.

Those years contained some of the happiest moments of my life and the saddest events of my life. It was all that death that I experienced that gave me a glimpse of the deep pain and injury I caused my victim's family. But that realization was still yet to come. To that point in my life, this series of deaths caused a lingering sadness that outweighed the happiness. It was those sorrowful memories that seemed to change everything. Little did I know, I had a short period of freedom before I would make the worst decision of my life and that decision would end yet another life. That decision would end my own life as I knew it as well, causing me to be locked up with a sentence nearly twice as long as I had even existed.

A CHANGE IN FAMILY FORTUNE

W e moved from my aunt's house to a house in Riverside. It was a four-bedroom house with one and a half baths. It had spacious back and front yards with trees and plenty of shade. It was a lovely house, not as sweet as Lydia's house, but much nicer than our home in Apple Valley. This new 'hood' was a reflection of my Apple Valley neighborhood. It was mostly black residents, with a smaller population of Hispanics. I was one of a handful of whites that hung out there, but I was quickly accepted and treated like anyone else.

My parent's newfound prosperity enabled us to take extended vacations to the world-renowned theme parks such as SeaWorld, Knotts Berry Farm, Six Flags, and Disneyland. We also visited exciting places such as Las Vegas, with all its glitz and fanfare. Colorado and its rocky terrain was fun because these were family events. In Colorado, Chris and I made off from the tours and did our own thing. We bought weed and tripped off the mountains and rivers. We gelled with the down-to-earth people, who were so much more open and approachable than back home. The girls were ten times hotter and down for anything! Those were times I cherish to this day, my first-ever trip to such fun-filled wonder worlds and, unfortunately, my last. Little did I know then, but I would never own a car, apply for a driver's license, or earn my first paycheck. I would never write a check or legally buy alcohol or vote. Man, I never even went shopping on my own, or graduated from high school (at least in the conventional sense, walking the stage in a non-correctional setting), or took a girl on a date. As I write this, at age twenty, I still have so much to see and learn.

DANIEL'S USE OF WEED & COPING
WITHOUT IT

D rugs were my weakness. They were my road to destruction, a path I chose, though I would never have imagined the total ruin they would lead me to. I regret ever being introduced to drugs. Looking back, I don't know if my life would have been much different, though. I was introduced to drugs at a very young age and drugs seemed to be the pastime of everyone I knew; drugs of one type or another, were the passion of my friends.

For some, television, music, or even video games were enough of a distraction from the realities of life. For me, not one of these activities helped because I would still stress. I would be bombarded with thoughts on my troubles. While these activities were a distraction, they weren't enough of a distraction. Weed, on the other hand, actually took my mind away. Weed sent me to bliss, and no matter what was happening around me, I wasn't there. No problem was ever bigger than the escape that weed promised and faithfully delivered.

My appreciation of nature also made the perfect marriage for getting high. The awesome sensation of being outdoors, particularly at parks, amplified the high. Parks were my preferred place to go to get high. The feeling of the wind blowing against my skin as my mind drifted into the abyss was incomparable to anything else I had yet experienced in my young life. I was hooked. The scent of the trees, mixed with the summer heat, or the smell of spring, made for my personal paradise. The soft grass and the inviting tranquility of the park atmosphere was the best experience in the world to me, at least that's how I saw it at the time.

Looking back, weed was my primary addiction. I thought I needed weed to survive. I breathed weed (with each inhale) for dear life. And it was this feeling of desperation that ultimately led me to murder.

But before that extreme, I risked everything to keep drugs flowing in and out of my life. Through buying low and selling high, I could afford all the weed I felt I needed. The risk was selling out of my parents' home. I never realized they could have lost the house. The cities, states, and feds have all of these drug forfeiture laws that could have landed us on the streets again. We could have been homeless. I also sold it at school. Luckily, no one dimed me out as the girl did about the BB gun.

I wasn't rich, but I earned enough not to need anything. I bought guns, clothes, fancy shoes, and watches. I looked out for Chris and my other brothers. I bought my mom gifts and helped with groceries. And, of course, I bought a lot of weed. I earned about $600 to $900 a week, sometimes more.

✖ ✖ ✖

MENTORS and a few self-help classes that I have taken have

taught me about addiction in general and have helped me understand my personal and insatiable addiction to weed. I didn't even know people could get addicted to weed. I knew people that were hooked on meth, on coke, like Tiffany, as well as on smack (heroin), but I never imaged that I could be addicted to weed. I know better now.

It was a hard adjustment in prison. When I was first locked up in juvie, I saw how available drugs were on the inside. Prison is no different than anywhere. Drugs flow through the security walls and over the razor wire like water. Prison doesn't isolate people from drugs. I have had to learn to live without weed. I had to make a decision. One thing that helped me refuse weed in prison is the price. Weed and all drugs in prison cost three to five times the street price. I also learned by the examples around me that going into drug debt in prison can be more costly in other areas, besides financial. Drugs are probably the number one reason for violence in prison. I made my mind up not to be a statistic again. Being in prison for life was enough of a statistic for me.

Classes like the Men For Honor's "Helping Youth Offenders Understand Their Harm" (Helping Y.O.U.T.H) taught me positive coping skills to replace the negative coping mechanism I was using through weed. The truth was, I just didn't know how to cope with the hardships of life. Weed was not only my escape, but my track and field to run as fast and as far away from life's challenges as possible. Through weed, I learned to simply run from my problems, not face and confront them.

Helping Y.O.U.T.H. helped me to learn healthy coping skills such as talking to other people and playing sports as a way to de-stress. When I first heard this approach, it made perfect sense. Sports was the only other activity I could do that would completely take me away from my problems. The only difference was that sports didn't put me in that state of bliss that I used to love so dearly. That state of bliss fit neatly into my cool and calm personality. Weed gave me that extreme state of relaxation that my character mirrors. Sports had the opposite effect. Sports amped me up, made me want to go. Sports showed me what I was made of and offered a challenge I enjoyed. Helping Y.O.U.T.H. helped me see life's challenges in the same way, and helped me view life difficulties as events to be overcome through effort and courage. I related to the word courage because that word is the word I learned early on through my brother, Chris. To face problems as conquerable challenges, and to do so with courage makes sense to me – now. Unfortunately, these concepts and approaches were not taught to me earlier in life. I first had to make the worst decision of my entire life, and then come to a place where I was forced to confront my bad choices, my past way of life, and the ways that I viewed the world.

I am now learning to think things out and avoid impulsive behavior. I now know the difference between anti-social behavior and pro-social actions. I lived a life of taking. I was a drain on society's resources because of my reckless behavior and destructive attitude. That didn't mean that I was worthless, as I often thought I was. It just meant that I wasn't living up to my potential as a human being. It seemed no one I hung around with was living up to his potential. We were just existing and not really contributing or trying to be anything positive.

As I am mentored, I am learning to support and mentor other people. My assigned job here on the grounds is as an aide for prisoners under the Americans with Disabilities Act. My job is to push those in wheelchairs around to their destinations on the compound. I help them transport their canteen purchases, deliver their food trays, and help them clean their cells. All of this interaction helps me relate to people in pro-social ways. I have learned that there is also a positive sensation that comes with helping people; it feels good. It feels good to be needed and it feels good to be appreciated. This job has offered me a small way to give back. These experiences are helping me understand how larger society works and what it means to live a pro-social life. My less fortunate, disabled peers have also indirectly shown me how much worse things could be.

There's no question that prison is a miserable place; it was designed to be a miserable place. Yet, despite the slight curvature in my spine, I can still give 'em heck on the basketball and hand-ball courts. I am entirely able-bodied and that is something I am learning not to take for granted. I am also healthy, in mind, and body. Since I have been in prison, I have seen guys die of cancer and other incurable sicknesses. Being in prison is miserable, but I can't even imagine how miserable being in prison with a fatal disease would be.

I was sentenced to life before the age of maturity. They gave me a sentence of 26 years-to-life before I could fathom what that meant. It's hard to imagine something I haven't even lived yet. I'm only 20-years-old as I write my story now. So that "forever" sentence, to me, represents a type of hopelessness. What does it mean for a teen to be sentenced to forever? It's like being sentenced to a pitch-black room and told to make it around as best I can. I imagine that is also what it feels like to be sentenced to die by nature from a fatal disease. I'd rather search my way around the room in the dark, with the slim chance of finding a door, a window, or some other way out. So in that sense, I have hope. I can't see it, I can't feel it, but with the positive coping skills I am learning, I have the strength to see it through, to fight the good fight.

In all honesty, I still get tempted by weed. It seems so natural as if God put it here for our use and pleasure. Yet, the murder I committed under the influence of weed is a reminder of what I am capable of when I'm high. That is scary because the last thing I want to do is harm anyone else. This fear is the most prevalent deterrent to me as far as getting high. It just isn't worth it. The pain, the sorrow and the hell I put my victim's family through, and my community, and my family, just isn't worth it.

DANIEL'S SENSELESS MURDER

The pain, the sorrow, and the hell that I described above takes me to that fateful day in 2014. It was the day I acted cold-blooded, against an angel. It was a fall day, a warm and beautiful day that I callously killed. I was barely sixteen years old. I was hanging out with Anthony, who was two years younger than me, and a neighborhood friend I had known for only a few months. We were at my favorite place, the nearby park in Riverside. Anthony and I were sitting on a bench getting high, as we had done many times before, though we should have been in school.

I had been away from home for days, nearly a week. I was afraid to go home because of the fury I would face after I left the house in shambles. I had been partying that night and lost track of time. My parents were out and were supposed to be out until late. That gave me the nerve to party, hard. Like all good parties, the house got kind of messed up, well, a lot messed up. The house was in shambles! While high, I still was able to recognize that my parents were pulling up in the driveway. There was no way I was going to be able to clean up the huge mess I had made before they walked through the front door, but I did have time to hit the back door before they knew I was just there seconds ago.

I decided to hang out with Marlo, the neighborhood drug dealer. I had only known her for a few months, but she was cool and we clicked. She took a liking to me because we used to joke around and have fun. I told her that I needed to "hang out" with her for a few days because I didn't have nowhere else to go. Marlo was an attractive older black American woman. She was fearless, probably because she had the backing of her gang, plus she had heart. With me, she had no reason to have her guard up. I didn't seem like a threat. And to be honest, I wasn't a threat, until that day, until that moment when I became desperate for more weed. I am sure she would never have imagined that letting me live with her and allowing me to see some of her weed stashes was the worst decision she ever made.

I call it that "fateful day" because looking back, it was inevitable. If I didn't kill Marlo, I would have killed someone, if not myself. I think back to the bullet game on the railroad tracks. Any one of us could have been killed, not to mention an innocent person. I think back to the day I was lured to the park by Wendy's boyfriend. Had I had a gun that day, I would have been on trial for his murder, not Marlo's. He just wanted to fight and though I genuinely believe they would have jumped me, the most dangerous weapons they had were their hands. For me, it was all about gunplay. I wanted a gun so bad that day I could taste it. It hurt my ego to have to talk my way out of that threatening situation. They brought it to me and I wanted to give it back to them, but ten times worse. Me, against the three of them, just wasn't going to work. Me, and a gun against three of them, would have evened up the odds. I would have had no problem with dusting any of them.

That's not to say that I had a problem with fighting, but with the odds against me, guns are the answer. Either way, I had a killer mentality early on. I never stopped to think of it that way, but that is the reality of it. What I've learned from the classes I've taken is that I had a fatalistic/apathetic attitude. I didn't care if I died and I didn't care about others. While Marlo offered me empathy by allowing me to stay with her, I responded with complete disregard for her and what she did for me. It was that attitude that allowed me to shelve the love and care my parents were trying to express through their actions, including their chastisement when I went sideways. I didn't see it or understand it then, and now I'm finally coming to terms with that.

I am forever stuck with the memory of knocking on Marlo's door with Anthony by my side. We were returning from getting high at the park. I could hear Marlo on the other side of the door looking through the peephole to see who it was. Like always, she opened the door with a welcoming smile, turned her back to us, and walked back across the tan carpet to resume her seat on the couch. Anthony and I followed close behind. We wanted more weed but I had no more money. I was too shy to ask for a front since I was already staying at her house. I guess it's weird to say that I didn't want to impose, but had no problem slamming a bottle over her head and fighting with Marlo as I tried to rob her. Anthony just stood there in shock.

No surprise that she fought back and viciously, too. I guess she sensed her life depended on it because that's how she fought back. Weed twisted my thoughts so much that I was attacking the one person in the neighborhood that trusted me to live with her; I think she would have given me anything. Smoking weed just before and days with little sleep took me to another reality, a false reality.

I felt absolutely nothing as I tried my best to subdue her. As we fought, Anthony continued to stand there in silence. I think he was surprised that I was acting on his earlier joke that we rob her. It was at that point that I pulled out my hunting knife and I stabbed Marlo. High on weed and high on adrenaline, I not only stabbed her once, but I stabbed her again and again. I stabbed her until she stopped fighting me. I stabbed her until she stopped breathing. I felt bad at that point, but I felt like it was her fault, because she was fighting me. (I didn't understand then that blaming others was one of my character defects. It was just another one of my harmful coping mechanisms.)

We searched all of Marlo's stashes and we walked out of there with a couple of ounces. I also took her cell phone. We then locked the door and we left. We headed back to the park. I cleaned up, threw some clothes away, and sported my undershirt for the rest of the day. I ditched all of the evidence, except for the phone. I felt completely numb. Any thoughts of regret were quickly pushed out. I smoked more weed.

As the weeks went by, I tried not to think about what we had done. I continued to be completely apathetic, disconnected, and removed from my actions. I just didn't care. I didn't think about the consequences, not only of getting caught, but of the full effect my actions would have on my victim's family, Anthony, the community, and my family. It didn't matter that it was Anthony's idea; what mattered was that I acted on it.

Approximately two weeks later, while at a home girl's house, Eve, I was talking on Marlo's phone with another girl. The girl and I were playing and joking and just having fun. My fun was interrupted by an aggressive knock on the door. I peeped out the window and was surprised to see cops everywhere! Black and whites, big flat black trucks, all flashing their emergency lights. Many of the swarm of officers were sporting their typical blue uniforms, but there were others dressed in all black jumpsuits and full tactical gear. Their guns were drawn and pointed toward the house. At that point, I knew it was over. The temptation to run out the back quickly died out. "They are everywhere," I thought. I surrendered.

It was the first time I had ever been arrested. I was still numb. I was taken to the Riverside Police Department and dragged through the long booking process. I never saw or heard anything of Anthony, but during the arraignment, they seemed to know the whole story. They didn't ask me anything initially. I was charged with murder/robbery, which carries the death penalty.

I was shocked that they were trying to give me the death penalty. I never thought the stakes were that high. I knew robbing Marlo was wrong, and I knew I could get in trouble, but "trouble" was abstract to me then. I thought it was like it was in school, where they just kicked me out of school or something like that.

In the end, I was too young for the death penalty, and the district attorney wanted to make things easier for Marlo's family and on me. He offered a deal of 26 years to life. Again, I had no idea what that meant, but my lawyer said it was a good deal. I knew it was better than the death penalty. The whole process took a few months. Today I would describe my sentence as a quarter-century, which makes it sound as serious as it is. I was also ordered to pay restitution, $15,000—more money than I had ever seen in my life.

12

YOUTH AUTHORITY

I was seventeen-years-old when I was finally sent to Youth Authority, juvenile hall. I was scared. I kept thinking about elementary and how cruel kids can be. I was tired of fighting and I definitely didn't want to kill anyone else. After I pled guilty, I knew I was going to be sent to Y.A., but I didn't know what to expect at Y.A.

The thing is, I could never have expected what Y.A. turned out to be. In a word, it was fun! The kids were wild, the staff was wild, and the whole experience was crazy. It was part co-ed, so we got to see girls all the time. The girls shared recreation time with us. Recreation time was at the pool where we'd swim, wrestle, and race in the water. We'd do flips off the ledge and push each other in. We also got to hang out together in the grassy area under the trees and shade. It was kind of like a park only we couldn't leave. If we weren't in our sports clothes, we had to wear tan khakis and a white T-shirt. We also shared events on the field, like sports. It was really cool. I met quite a few girls, but I never forgot Ashley.

Y.A. also had weights and a movie room where we could get away from things for a while. Like the Big House, we were permitted contact visits with friends and loved ones. I was always happy to see my family, but the hard part was and still is when they had to leave. It was excruciating!

In Y.A., I felt ready to accept academic challenges. School was seven days a week, no girls. With that much schooling, I figured I might as well make the best of it. We had to be there; there was no ditching, so I did as the Romans do, I put the time in and actually did well. I paid attention to the teachers; I read the books and did the homework. I excelled enough to earn my General Equivalency Diploma (GED.) It was more of a relief than a joy. A relief to get past it and to know for sure that I could achieve academically.

Of course, I knew that, but I felt like I needed to prove it to everyone else. Plus, with the colossal disappointment that came with my arrest, I felt like I needed to give my mom something to prove my worth. All told, there wasn't much else to do in Y.A., except get in trouble. And I'd had enough of that.

When I say enough of trouble, I mean violence. There were a lot of melees and gang riots in Y.A. Anything could set off a fight - looking at someone from a rival neighborhood wrong, a memory of a perceived disrespect from the streets. Those were cause for "taking off on sight," as they used to say. I saw some guys get messed up in Y.A. The guys who showed fear and weakness were the targets and preyed upon regularly. The staff wore uniforms, carried mace, and had no problem using it to break up fights. It was almost routine. The staff either called us "wards" or "delinquents." The staff was also corrupt. Cash money was illegal; it was considered contraband. But we'd get it in one way or another so we could "buy" all types of things from the staff. If you can imagine it, it can be bought.

Y.A. was full of vices, and that was the fun part. It was the violence I wanted to avoid. For an institution of isolation, drugs were everywhere. Weed, ecstasy, heroin, and coke were in Y.A. By then, I had learned my drug of choice and stuck with it. Weed was my limit.

There were also a lot of contraband phones. We had flip phones back then. It was cool to talk to my mom and Ashley after the lights went out. We shared things like that. One phone was enough for a group of us. If we got caught, which some guys did, it wasn't a big deal. My time in Y.A. flew by. I spent just under a year in juvenile prison before being shipped to the Big House.

13

PRISON

"What am I doing here?" Was the question I asked myself the first day I woke up in county jail after leaving Y.A. That question followed by, "This sucks!" I have since been in prison for nearly five years. I began my stint at Chino, a reception center. Chino is a lower-level prison. Now, I am housed at the Progressive Programming Facility at California State Prison, Los Angeles. I am told that this facility is a lot more relaxed than the "gladiator schools" that represent a closer reality to prison life than here. Even so, I am locked up with a date pushed so far into the future that it seems light-years away. Right now, I cannot see the difference. The bottom line is that I lost my freedom, or better said, I forfeited my freedom, ever so careful to take responsibility for my deeds. That is what the self-help classes teach - it begins with taking personal responsibility.

As expected, I have my good days and I have my bad days. Some days I simply do not feel like being in prison. Other days I don't feel like being searched and felt on by the various officers who are looking for "whatever they can find." And I have never dealt with so many personalities. Guys who are always in a bad mood or guys who are just backward in every way or guys who think they are the police, though their prison blues are just as blue as mine. Still, whether good or bad, each day is a mirror to the next: get up at 5:30 a.m., walk to the mess hall, wait for breakfast, work, dayroom, lights out. Throw in some classes here and there, a few medical visits, and a random lockdown for one reason or another, and that is prison. Since the days bleed into one another with hardly any deviation, the best way I keep up with the days of the week is to remember what is for breakfast each day. Monday it's pancakes, my favorite. At one point, they were calling me "Pancake" because I could take down so many in one sitting. I love those things! Tuesday, it's eggs and so forth.

Race wise, prison isn't much different from the neighborhoods I was raised in. For the most part, prison is black and brown. On the yard, we come in with our twisted mentalities. The classes help us transform ourselves. This yard, the Progressive Programming Facility, is exceptional. I am told of the racial divisions, the stabbings, and widespread gang violence that infest the other facilities. Guys get themselves in trouble with drug debts that can only be paid in one of two ways: the money or a chunk of flesh. Other guys disrespect other races and their own race "disciplines" them to satisfy the offended race, so a racial war doesn't grow out of it. While there are occasional fistfights on the PPF, the warrior type of frequent violence that happens on the other facilities is absent here.

Still, it takes time to shed negative ways. When I first came in, like most, the dark stories about prison had me mentally prepared for life or death battles. Kill or be killed was the mentality I adopted. Thankfully, it isn't quite like that. At least not here on the PPF.

I did get into one minor scuffle about a year ago. The guy approached me in a foul manner and we traded punches. It happened just like that! The truth is, I never really liked him from the beginning. I lost 61 days of good-time credit for that one. Not much of a disincentive when you're facing life anyhow. Still, I want to do better. I have to do better. It is my aim to get myself fit for society. That's the hardest thing about prison, you have to be locked up, but you want to be free.

My biggest challenge is trying to shake my aversion to authority. I've managed to tame that part of my nature, but it rears up in an awful way when other prisoners try to tell me what to do. There are times when prisoners lead groups or programs that benefit us, but they don't all know how to talk to people and when they approach me in a foul way, I get triggered. Since that is a real problem for me, I pulled back on those programs for now. The way I see it, I am a work in progress and I have plenty of time to work on myself, a lifetime! There are other character defects I can work on while putting that issue to the side. When I am better able to master my coping skills, which takes practice, then I can allow other guys to test me. But for now, to keep from hurting anyone else, I want to acknowledge my weaknesses and proceed with caution.

These days, I write poetry in my cell. I enjoy that. I read fiction books that take me out of this place for a while. I'm thinking of signing up for a correspondence college course. I'll take one class at a time and see how that goes.

14

REGRETS & REMORSE

I will begin this part of my story, focusing on my regrets, by stating that I am glad I got caught. Had I not been caught, I likely would have hurt others or ended up dead myself. I was fairly charged. Had I been sentenced to life without the possibility of parole, I would certainly have earned it. I pled guilty immediately and received mercy with my plea deal. That didn't feel good at the time, but I am proud of accepting responsibility then, though I didn't know or understand half of what I do now. That said, I can't say it enough, prison is a miserable place. Even so, with the help of friends and mentors here, and my family's support outside, I can see my transformation. I can see growth in areas like how I deal with people and the empathy I have gained for others. I am more patient and drugs are not my motivation. I have a long way to go, but I am progressing, not stagnant.

I cannot waste this opportunity not to apologize for the many people I have victimized and the extreme misery I have caused others. I compare this situation to a darkened house. In this house, I can see all of the people I have hurt and disappointed. Their faces are like needles pointing back at me, piercing my skin.

I feel shame and sincere regret. My regrets go back to when I was a kid. I have made bad decisions almost all of my life. This house is a reminder of those bad decisions. It is a very rude awakening.

Now with a more sober mind, I am learning not to run from the horrific act of murder I committed against Marlo Williams. I take full responsibility for my actions. I wish that I had never gotten involved with drugs. I wish that I had done better in school. I wish that I had made a lot better choices back then. But here I am now, in this horrible reality. I am trying to face my reality as best and courageously as possible.

I miss my family and that is the worst. That includes Ashley. We talk every other day and the occasional visits only make me wish for more. The phone calls are limited to fifteen minutes, which makes saying good-bye excruciating. Same with the visits, which amount to about three to four hours on weekends, when my family can come. Saying good-bye is like being torn apart each time. I learn to live with it. At least I am alive.

I think about Marlo Williams often. She was the motivation behind my willingness to participate in this project. I needed to come clean. Writing about the details of the day that I murdered was very difficult. I wrestled with that part for days, crying in silence with just a few sentences at first, and then going to sleep because it was all so emotionally draining. Killing someone and then trying to transform from such a horrible act is simply exhausting.

DOCKET D073276

COURT BACKGROUND ON DANIEL DAVIDSON & ANTHONY E,
MURDER OF MARLO WILLIAMS

05-10-2018

BACKGROUND

Fifteen-year-old Anthony E. and 16-year-old Daniel Davidson
murdered Marlo Williams in the course of robbing her of
marijuana.

Police found Williams' dead body on the floor of her apartment
on December 23, 2014, a week after she was killed. She was lying
in a large pool of blood. Williams had been stabbed well over 50
times, on her head, torso, arms and legs. The stab wounds pene-
trated her right and left lungs, right liver, right kidney,
diaphragm, and colon. She had also suffered blunt force injuries
on both the right and left temples of her forehead that caused
internal bleeding.

The police determined that Williams' cell phone was being used
by Davidson. Officers contacted Anthony E. after interviewing
Davidson. Anthony E. admitted that he had been to Williams'
apartment to buy marijuana from her, but denied any participa-
tion in the murder and robbery. He was taken to the police

station and advised of his Miranda rights. The officers told Anthony E. that Davidson said that Anthony E. had killed Williams. Anthony E. then admitted that he and Davidson were at Williams' apartment and that he helped Davidson kill Williams.

Anthony E. said that Davidson hit Williams over the head without warning or provocation, then grabbed a knife from the kitchen and stabbed her repeatedly. Davidson then told him to choke Williams, because she was not dying despite the multiple stabbings. Anthony E. put his hands on Williams' neck and choked her. He estimated that he choked her for about 30 seconds.

Davidson told Anthony E. to get another knife from the kitchen because he could not kill Williams with the first knife. Anthony E. brought Davidson a second knife, and then another knife when the second one did not do the job. Davidson repeatedly stabbed Williams with the knives. Anthony E. denied ever stabbing Williams, but admitted that, in addition to choking her, he punched Williams twice, trying "to knock her out" because she kept thrashing and resisting.

After Williams was subdued, Anthony E. ransacked the apartment looking for marijuana. He found no large cache. Anthony E. stole the 14 or 15 grams of marijuana that were in her bedroom. Before leaving the apartment, Anthony E. checked Williams' eyes to make sure she was dead.

Anthony E. said that several times, he, Davidson, and Anthony G. had talked about killing Williams and stealing her marijuana, but Anthony E. thought they were joking. He said he had no plan to rob Williams when he went to her apartment on December 17, and he did not intend to kill her. He instead blamed Davidson for the murder. Anthony E. said that he was scared when Davidson told him to strangle Williams, and that he "didn't think about it" when he put his hands on Williams' neck; he was just caught up in the moment. He also said, however, that he choked her "to get her to stop movin[g]" because he "wanted it to be over," and that he punched her to "knock her out."

Anthony G. was not charged in this case and is not a party to this appeal.

According to the presentence report, Davidson told the police that Anthony E. was the one who stabbed Williams over 50 times, and claimed that he, Davidson, "never touched [Williams]."

Anthony G. contacted the police to provide information shortly after he heard about the murder. He was 17 years old at that time. He testified that he, Anthony E., and Davidson visited with Williams about five or six times in December 2014 to smoke marijuana with her and to buy marijuana from her. On December 15 or 16, Anthony E., Davidson, and Anthony G. were smoking marijuana together. Davidson or Anthony E. brought up the subject of robbing and killing Williams. Anthony G. refused to participate. The other two said they were joking and dropped the subject.

The Riverside County District Attorney directly filed criminal charges against Anthony E. in the superior court, charging him with murder, robbery, and the special circumstance of committing the murder during the course of a robbery. (Pen. Code, §§ 187, subd. (a), 190.2, subd. (a)(17)(A) & 211.) A jury found Anthony E. guilty of the charges, and found true the special circumstance. On August 26, 2016, the trial court sentenced Anthony E. to a term of 25 years to life in state prison for murder, pursuant to sections 190 and 190.5, and imposed and stayed under section 654, subdivision (a) the upper term of six years for robbery.

Davidson was charged as a codefendant in the complaint and information. He pleaded guilty to first degree murder and admitted the allegation that he had personally used a deadly weapon. The court sentenced Davidson to a determinate term of one year in prison for the enhancement and a consecutive indeterminate term of 25 years to life.

THE HARDKNOCK LIFE

1

YOUTH

My name is Curtis Frazier. I was convicted of attempted murder in 2006 and sentenced to twenty-one years with 85% in 2009.

I recall my life growing up as a child in East Oakland as always being crazy. As far back as I can remember I lived in poverty-stricken areas with a criminally minded environment. I was taken away from my mother at nine years old due to me not going to school and committing crimes. I always had abandonment issues. My mother tried her hardest she just couldn't keep me. I was too much for her back then because I stayed in trouble.

I was in special education classes while in school. It used to be an embarrassment for me and I believe that it made me act out in bad behavior when the kids used to tease me for being a slow learner. In school I was never paying attention because I had an attention disorder and learning never excited me so stealing becoming my hobby.

I started my career of stealing at age eight. I was always stealing from the local stores because I was so poor. I used to steal bicycles from different schools. I used to steal the bikes and sell them to the drug dealers in the neighborhoods until I got caught and went to juvenile hall.

When I went to juvenile hall for the first time I was scared and confused. However, when I was there I noticed that my attention was different. I was paying close attention to everything around me. They were going to release me but my mama didn't come get me.

I got used to going to juvenile hall after a while so much that they got used to seeing me too. They used to allow me to pick my side to do my time in—the good or the bad side.

My uncle and aunt gained custody of me at age nine but that made me worst. Psychologically I was messed up because I missed my mother. Living in the house with my aunt and uncle was the worst time in my life. That's when the worst things started happening to me. When I was staying with them they used to let me do a lot of things. That's when I met my first baby mama and had my first son, Curt Jr. That was about the best thing that came out of living there. I have nine baby mamas in total. That's a whole other story.

As far as living with my aunt and uncle and all the different kinds of abuses, abuses like sexual, verbal, and mental, it still affects me to this day. I do not want to describe the sexual abuse. My aunt was the worst to me though.

One day I came in the house five minutes late from my curfew and my aunty whooped me so bad with an extension cord that I couldn't go to school for five days. I had all kinds of welts on my face and neck. She used to verbally abuse me with the things she would say about my mother. My mother was addicted to crack cocaine. My aunt would always throw that up in my face. She would also talk about my disability as far as my slow learning abilities. My aunt and uncle would show favoritism towards their kids and treat me like I didn't belong. It made me feel depressed, sad, and lonely. I felt let down and abandoned.

They had two sons. The oldest one started using what we used to call grimmies. That's crushed cocaine in cigarettes. He and I never had a good relationship. The other son was around my age and we had a close bond. We fought like siblings sometimes but we were the closest of them all. I stayed with them for all of my teenage years.

I always went to jail there too. I went to jail a lot for drugs, stealing cars, and fights at school. My uncle used to come get me though, unlike my mama. I found out later that he only came to get me because he didn't want to lose that check he was receiving every month from the county just to keep me. The longest I stayed in jail as a youth was three years. That was in the California Youth Authority. I was 16 when I went in there for attempted murder. Yeah, I hadn't noticed that my crimes had elevated into more serious crimes until I had already committed them.

Those three years didn't help my path the least bit. I was fighting all the time in there too. That was where I experienced my first race riot. It was against the Southern Mexicans. I always knew I could fight but a riot is a different kind of fighting experience – it's scary!

When I got out of there it was all downhill. I got involved in a street gang and learned even more bad behaviors. In my neighborhood there was always some crimes happening. East Oakland in the '90s was full of crime-infested communities doing the same things, selling dope.

2

GETTING BY

My mother stayed on the dope spot where my brother's uncle hustled at. He needed a lookout and I stepped up for the job. He paid me four hundred dollars. I never looked back after that. Cold part is how my mother used to bring me sandwiches when I got hungry out there too. That was a trip.

From that I went and bought my first half-ounce of dope and started selling drugs for myself. I thought I was balling off my little half ounce. I had brought me a car, a bucket for 150 dollars. My little balling fantasy didn't last long though. My bucket blew up on me on the freeway.

Time passed and I was back and forth living with my mom and my uncle. One time I went to my aunt's house and she thought that she could put her hands on me again like she used to. I was listening to my music minding my own business and she started yelling at me about it. She hit me in the back of my head real hard because I was ignoring her. When she turned her back I grabbed a broom stick and busted her in the back of her head with the broomstick. When my uncle and his two sons heard about it they jumped me. I left there and never went back.

About a year later I had sold some drugs to a person and I didn't know that the money he gave me was fake until I went to buy something from the store. I was almost at my potna's house when the cops rolled up on me. I didn't know that the store clerk had called them on me for giving him some counterfeit money. That was my first time being arrested as an adult. I received twenty days and three years probation for counterfeit money.

When I got out I was doing real bad financially. I started strong arming people. My first strong arm robbery was when I robbed a white boy in Berkeley for about 75 dollars. I did it because I was hungry and I didn't have anything to eat. I didn't have no other way of knowing how to earn money. Strong arming people became my way to eat. I was so focused on strong arming people that I ended up robbing my own relative.

I had just come out from spending the night at a girl's house and I had to go meet my baby's mama to talk about our kid. It was early in the morning. I got sidetracked and walked up to 82nd and MacArthur to hang out and kick it. I ran into one of my high school potnas from Castlemont High School. He had told me that there was a group of kids in the back of the school shooting dice. It was my intention to rob the winner but when we got to the dice game I was just watching. There was one youngster with some Jordans on his feet and some Penny Hard-aways (shoes) around his neck. I wanted those Pennys real bad! I looked down at my feet and saw that I had on some scuffed up old K-Swiss. Those shoes he had only been out for about two weeks! I asked him if I could see them and he let me see them. I had them in my hand to check the size. I told my potna that I was about to get them shoes.

All of a sudden the bell rung for class. Everybody started splitting up. I got close to the youngster and I hit him with a two-piece combo that dropped him to the ground. The school patrol saw us and they came and chased us off. I ran to my uncle's house to shave and clean myself up. I put the shoes on my feet and in my stupidity, I went back up to Castlemont High School to meet my baby's mama. I had been warned that I shouldn't go back up there by my potna but I didn't listen.

I was approached by the dude whose shoes they were, his brother, and his uncle. Fortunately for me, the uncle knew me. That didn't prevent the youngster from not wanting to get his shoes back and I didn't want to give them back so he and me fought. I was scuffed up too. The uncle held me down so the youngster could get his shoes. He took them right off my feet. While I was there the school police caught me and took me to jail for taking them shoes. I received a year in the county jail for robbery.

When I got out I found out that I had robbed a family member. I was at my cousin's house and she told me that some of my family was coming to see me. When the door opened it was the youngster I had robbed for the shoes and two other family members. When we found out that we were family we all laughed about all that.

By this time I was 20 years old and over experienced in the crime department. It was around 1998 when I had met a girl on the bus. She let me know that she had a boyfriend and he was in jail but she did not tell me that he was crazy. After about 6 months of knowing her I had popped up at her house and that's when I met her boyfriend. She and me had a big argument on her porch and he went into the house. I didn't know why but I played it smart and I left.

I saw him later on with some of his homeboys and since nothing was said I thought that we had squashed the beef. Then I saw him about six months later when I was on the spot. He pulled up on me and I didn't notice him until he spoke to me. He said that he wanted to holla at me when he came out of the store. I didn't trip but I had a funny feeling so I went to go get my potna.

Me and dude talked like it was cool but when my potna left me, dude pulled out a gun and tried to rob me. I gave him my radio and tried to run and that's when he shot me in my chest. The bullet came out my arm.

I ran to my cousin's house who I was living with and fell out on the floor. She called the ambulance and they came and got me. I stayed about three days in the hospital because it was only a flesh wound. When I got out I was so mad I went looking for that dude. Lucky for him that I didn't find him.

I went back to selling dope on the spot and I had to stay with a gun so I wouldn't get caught slipping no more. When I did get caught slipping it was by the police. This time when I went to jail, the case was much more serious. It was guns and dope. I went to the pen. The big house. After a long fight in court I got sentenced to three years with 85%. I ended up doing the maximum time because I had a lot of fights.

3

PRISON

One fight I had while I was in prison I threw some scalding hot coffee in the face of this dude. He didn't know what hit him until I got through beating on him. We was bunkies on the two yard, out of prison levels one to four. Four is the roughest. He was tripping on me. He tried to take his issues that he was having with his wife out on me.

We had two fights and he had beat me up the first time prior to the hot coffee incident and I was gonna accept it at first but he continued calling me a bitch and that's what set me off. That's when I cheated and threw the coffee on him. He shouldn't of been bragging that way. One of the worst things you can call a man in prison is a bitch.

I went to the hole behind that because he snitched on me. In order to not get charged in court for an assault I had to take a plea deal and they took all my good behavior time away from me.

When I got out of the hole after about 120 days I was being cool. Vacaville prison was a place that I could be cool at and just go home from, so I did.

4

PAROLED

I paroled and was homeless because I didn't have a place to go. All of my family did not want to deal with me while I was on parole. My family was all on section 8 low income housing. They would lose their low income housing if I got caught living with them.

About a month later I was able to go live with my daughter's mother in Richmond. When I was at her house it was like being in jail all over again. It was worst matter of fact. We had a lot of arguments and fights over the smallest issues. I would let her win the fights though.

Everything got crazy one time when we had a fight. I had grabbed her shirt and she called the police on me and put it on thick in front of the police like I hurt her bad. I did a violation in prison behind that. When I got out my stupid ass went right back to her. She did the same thing again too. Just what I deserved.

I got out and I went right back to her again like a dummy. This time when I went to jail and got out my family sent me to Louisiana so I would stay away from my baby's mama. I needed that too or my dumb ass would have went right back to her crazy ass again.

When I was in Louisiana things wasn't all good for me there neither. My mama had moved out there and she had her own problems. When I first got off of the greyhound bus I was picked up by my auntie and she started telling me about my mother's boyfriend and how bad he treated my mom and my brothers and sisters. Once I was settled in I did a little investigation on my own. What I found out was that all that my aunt had told me was true. He was a bad person and I wanted to see him about it. I wanted to beat his ass.

My mother was so in love with that dude that when she found out that I wanted to see him, she knew what I wanted to see him about. So she hid him from me so I couldn't get to him. But after about four months of being out there things had become easier for me to do.

My mother's boyfriend had called the house one day and I answered the phone. I befriended him by being nice. I asked him why he hadn't come to see me yet. He came out to see me that very same day. That dude was riding one of them little girl ten speed bicycles. I said to myself, "This a bootsie ass dude." That first impression of him I had was not good. He was ancient. My mother was mad about him coming over when I was there but she allowed him to stay overnight. I guess she missed him.

The next morning I woke up to cook breakfast for the entire family. When it was ready I called everybody down to come eat. When my mother's boyfriend appeared in the kitchen, he had on nothing but his t-shirt and drawls. I asked him nicely could he go put on some pants because there were females in the house. This fool's balls were sticking out of his drawls too. I flashed after he told me that he wasn't and he even had the nerve to tell me that I couldn't tell him what to do. My mother tried to tell him to listen but it was too late. I was already on top of that fool beating the brakes off his ass. He got me in a headlock somehow and my brother grabbed a cast iron skillet and let off some steam he had been holding in for a long time. My brother cracked him over the head with it. Me and my brother ended up jumping the dude that day. My mama was so mad at me that she sent me back to California. When I got back to Cali, I got in some more trouble that sent me back to the county jail.

When I got back I was homeless for a while. I had an old beat up Toyota and I used to sleep in my car. I started back selling drugs again and was making a little money. I elevated cars to a box Chevy. After a while I fixed it up and put music in it.

One day when I was grinding, selling drugs, on the block and this pretty girl had walked by and I was interested in her. So I got at her. We started dating and having sex. After a while we became in love, so I thought. The spot was rolling and money was coming fast. I used to let her keep my money and guns in her house while I was on the turf. I was the older guy on the block and the youngsters used to listen to me.

Police got up on our spot and they started coming through harassing us.

One day while I was driving down the block the police got behind me. By now my girl was pregnant and she stayed in the house. When I got jacked by the police I forgot that I had a gun and drugs on me. They pulled me over and did a four-way search clause on me. That's a probation or parole search. They found the drugs and gun. Since I was cool and didn't put up a fight they allowed me to relay a message to my girl for her to come pick up my car before they towed it away. When she brought her pregnant self around the corner crying they allowed me to kiss her and talk to her for a second. After she calmed down she drove off with my music playing loud in my car.

5

FIGHTING IN PRISON

I went to Santa Rita County Jail. That's the jail that houses everybody from Alameda County. When I went there me and some of my potnas from my hood formed our own little click inside of jail. When in jail everybody forms clicks for protection against those who might want to cause you harm if they see that you are a loner. So to prevent that from happening to us, me and some of my folks had banded together.

There was this prison click there, that I won't mention, who had run the prison and was most deepest in the prisons and jails. They had the most people with them. Me and my folks were not giving no fair fights. No one-on-one fights. You fight one of us you have to fight us all. This particular day is why I hate those prison click dudes til this day.

One of my folks had got into it with one of those dudes over a card game. They had supposed to have squashed the beef, I thought, but when day room came my folks had walked by dude and some of his potnas. My potna bumped dude so hard it made him fall over. Dude got up and challenged my potna to a fight, which they had. My potna had won and all of dude's potnas was gonna let it go because the fight was fair until I went up to dude's bunk area and grabbed all of his things and threw them over the rail yelling "Dude's gotta roll up!" What did I do that for?

Dude and his potnas came to see what was going on and to confront the issue. They surrounded us. Some of my folks who I thought was solid had left me there with two other potnas. They left us for dead. Dude and his potnas didn't get a chance to do anything because the officers stormed the pod in their riot gear.

The police came running in the pod searching everybody because they had seen what was about to happen. They came straight to me saying, "You don't roll nobody up! We do the rolling up around here." They took me to the multi-purpose room which we called the cold room.

I was in there relaxing at first until they cut that air conditioning on and I was left to suffer in the cold for about almost the entire night. When they finally came to get me they took me to the other side of the building to another pod. This pod had a bunch of those prison click dudes inside it and they had already received word that I was coming from one of their messengers.

While I was making my bed they approached me and asked if I was involved in that mess on the other side with one of their folks. I denied it. What? I ain't stupid. I saw that they were deep and plus they had a few big dudes on their team. Fortunately, for me I had knew this dude name V. He was their shot caller at the time. He was the dude who told them what to do. When they asked him what should they do with me, I had yelled up to his cell and told him who I was. I had to remind him but he remembered after a while and told them to sit on the situation until tomorrow. I thought I was alright but I was wrong.

While I was reading my bible one of the dudes came with a guy about a little bit bigger than me and told me that I had to fight him to even the score. I accepted the challenge. While we were walking to the place to fight I noticed two big dudes walking behind me. So when dude who I was supposed to fight turned around I hit him first and was getting the best of him. I had cracked his back. When his potnas heard him yell for help they came and started beating me up unmercifully. They were getting me good until another one of their homeboys came to save me. He told them to mind the orders they had received from their potna V and told them they were in violation. The one who saved me gave me an option: that was that I had to roll up. I thought about staying because rolling up affected my pride but instead I walked and pushed the button to the gate and told the officer that I had to leave. Ever since that fight I have been hating those guys because they jumped me.

When I went to Vacaville prison that incident trailed me there. I had become cool with some of them dudes that were in that prison click. They were from my city so they took me under their wing. They watched out for me and made sure that none of their folks did anything to me. They protected me. When them prison click dudes tried to confront me with that old stuff my new potna Black spoke up for me and told them that the issue was dead now and leave it alone once and for all. I was so glad because I was tired of that situation following me everywhere I went in prison. From there on out that issue was over but my stay in prison was not better. I was involved with more and more fights, with other races too and that's a no no.

✖ ✖ ✖

IN PRISON you are not supposed to get into with other races. The first time I had got into it with the Mexicans they were from up North, Northern California. There was this one who thought he was tough and used to pick on this older black man. One time he did it in front of me and I hit him in the mouth. I knew I was wrong, I know, but I couldn't just sit there and watch him bully on that old man anymore so we fought and almost caused a riot.

My black people were so mad at me for that. My next fight was with a Crip. He had bad words with my Bay Area potna. My Bay Area potna had some money and he didn't want to fight the dude but I did. I told my potna to just give me a can of chili and four soups. He said to go get it out of his locker and I did. The Crip dude got beat up for only 2 dollars and 50 cents.

My potnas got mad at me for that and they did what we call in prison a "DR," that's disciplinary punishment. I had to do 200 burpies in 2 hours. They did that to me because they said that my Bay Area potna needed to fight his own battles. Plus, I almost started a riot with the Crips that day.

Another dude named M was my best friend in prison. He worked in the prison. He would always tell me that he was getting into it with this older dude. One day he told me to come to the bathroom with him for him to show me something. When he unwrapped his arm he had a hole in his arm. The older dude had stabbed him with an ink pen for playing music too loud. He told me that the guy and another dude came to confront him. The older dude was with the prison gang. I told my potna that I was gonna come beat up the dude the next day. After I got off work I went to his dorm and confronted the dude and it got out of control. We ended up fighting.

The prison gang dude relayed a message to my potnas there and they had enough of my acting out. They told me that I had to leave if I kept getting into trouble and risking their freedom. I stayed out of trouble for a year. By then it was time for me to parole and I paroled successfully.

6

THE HARD KNOCK LIFE

I did a few more prison violations but eventually I got off parole. I went back to selling drugs and living the street life. One day I was going over to this spot to visit this female. I went to the corner store and I noticed this dude was eyeing me. He asked me did he know me and I said no you don't. He was sure that he did but I didn't have no time to react. Him and his homeboys started jumping me right there on the corner. To this day I don't know why dude did that to me. I left after people in the neighborhood had made sure I was ok. I left and plotted my revenge on dude but nothing turned up on that.

Since hustling was not for me I went back to what I was good at - I started robbing people again. It didn't pay as much as hustling and selling drugs did but it was something I liked doing. This one time I was walking down the street and this dude walked by me. I turned around and grabbed him by his neck and held him in a chokehold. When I went in his pockets he only had 14 dollars on him. I was so mad at myself for that. Life as a criminal has not been prosperous for me. When I look back on it all I see that it was a waste of time and missed opportunities.

I tried working at the Chevron refinery as a janitor. It was something that I wasn't used to but it kept me out of trouble for a minute. I had to thank my kid's mother for hooking me up with that but even while working there I just couldn't get rid of that bug inside of me. I just couldn't stop stealing.

I had built a rapport there with the boss and he liked me. One day he set a trap on me though. My position was a temporary position and the guy I stole from was trying to get me hired permanently but he tested me. He placed a stack of money in a coat that was hanging up in his office. I went through the coat and took a few bills out of the stack. The next day when I went to work dude asked me to come speak with him. Come to find out he had a hidden camera watching me when I stole the money.

He asked me about it and I lied. Dude gave me a chance to come clean but I didn't.

Eventually I went and told him the truth. He allowed me to repay him a portion back. Even so I had caught another violation and went to prison again. My education status was terrible and I guess that I just didn't have no training when it came to being depended on for legal work. While I was in prison the company I worked for had found out what happened and they gave the guy my last check to compensate for his loss.

On this new violation I went to Solano prison. My time there was smooth. I only had six months. While there though I saw a riot between the whites and the Southern Mexicans. I was so glad it didn't involve black people.

By now I was a seasoned criminal. It was the beginning of the 2000's. I had so many violations I could not remember every one. I know that I had been to prison around six or seven times by then.

When I got out of prison I was able to land another job. I had a new parole officer who made a few calls and got me hired at this recycling company. I was there for only two months. I got drunk one day and broke into my baby's mama house and jumped on her new boyfriend she had got while I was in prison. Plus I kicked him out of the house. She wasn't there.

When I left I was driving down the street and seen the dude walking. I rolled down the window and threatened him. I didn't notice Richmond police behind me. I tried to get away but they caught me. They didn't catch me for the crime until my baby's mama filed a police report on me. When my parole officer found out about it, it was a wrap. When I went to see my parole officer he immediately placed me under arrest. I went to Santa Rita County Jail. When they offered me a deal I refused it.

I went to what they call a Marsden hearing. In there you get to call character witnesses. Two people came on my behalf. When the hearing started I had to present my case. My parole officer walked in with my baby's mama at the end of the hearing. I felt that was a set up. My parole officer had proved to be against me. From there it went all bad. They charged me with assault, breaking and entering, and terrorist threats. That day was all bad. When they got ready to sentence me I had to speak up for myself. I eventually received a ten month violation and went to Folsom prison. I did the ten months and stayed out of trouble.

I have regrets sometimes for not getting my education while I have been wasting in prison. Maybe things would of worked out differently for my future.

When I got out I ran into the incident that led to the prison time I am now here at San Quentin for. The incident I never finished returned to haunt me. I ran into the dude who jumped me a while back. I couldn't believe the luck I was having. I didn't want him to see me so I pulled my car over around the corner. I was mad as the old school cartoon character Yosemite Sam. I walked up to dude and just started shooting. I thought I wouldn't remember or want revenge when I saw him but I couldn't hold it in. I didn't know if I shot him or not. All I remember is that I was shooting. Came to find out later I had shot the dude four or five times.

In that moment I felt liberated. The revenge was bittersweet. I knew I was wrong but I also knew that I wanted to make him hurt for what he had done to me. I left the scene and drove off like nothing had happened. When I went my place to relax I couldn't sleep. I was wondering if the dude had died or not. I watched the news and I listened to the chatter of the streets that night. Fortunately for me and him he didn't die.

I stayed on the run for about two weeks until they caught up with me. I was going to one of my uncle's houses and I didn't know that they had it under surveillance. My family was getting harassed for my wrong doing and the police had been aggressive with them. So once I got caught I was glad that they did catch me. I didn't want them to suffer any longer for my mistake.

I sat in the back of the police car thinking about what was going to happen to me. I knew this was a serious offense and I expected to do some serious time for it too. I got charged for attempted murder and sat in the county jail fighting the case for three years. Dude came to testify on me too. He was paralyzed and that made me look like a monster. Judges have sympathy for people like that. I had a public defender and I knew it wouldn't turn out good for me.

After the long wait and all the snitches that went against me I was sentenced to twenty-one years with 85%. They offered me thirty-five years to life as a deal at first. So when I think about it I can see the blessing in it. But still I didn't think that dude, who claimed to be a gangsta, would turn and snitch on me.

LIFE IN CALI PRISONS

When I got sentenced and came through the county to San Quentin I arrived at the reception part of the prison. That's where they place people when they are trying to determine where in California's prisons there is bed space available. I went to Salinas Valley, level four. They call it the killing zone. I was there for about two and a half years.

I quickly learned some discipline there. I got into it with this dude that was younger than me. We had an argument and I thought that I would fight him but when I found out that dude was the type who would stab you and that he had already stabbed a few people, I had to rethink that one.

Our argument was over the phone. They have this policy that if you place the phone down for five minutes the next person can use it. Once I found out that he was a hitter I quickly went and squashed the ordeal. Dude was a Crip and since I'm from the Bay that could of started a riot. That was the only time I was involved in anything there.

I saw a lot of riots though. The blacks and Mexicans were into it.

That feud went on for about a year and a half. Salinas Valley was a very dangerous place. Fortunately, I was not around when the riots were happening. I got transferred to Solano prison after I got my points down.

The prison points system works by a measure of zero to as high as you can make them. The higher your points the higher level of prison you will be in. Level four prison is the highest - one, two, three, four.

At Solano I became a porter and was responsible for cleaning the building I was in. I was doing ok at Solano until some dudes I knew from the streets came there. One of them was one of my little potnas and he was dope fiend. He was a little bitty dude with a big mouth and he thought he was the toughest dude on the yard because I was there. He knew that I had his back to the fullest so he would talk trash to other people and would run to me to back him up. Like a fool, I would.

This one time he had got into it with this dude over a dope debt and dude wouldn't pay him. I felt that the dude was taking advantage of him. I told my little potna that I would get his money for him. I confronted dude and dude gave me the money.

This other time my little potna had words with a dude twice his size and the dude wanted to fight. I ended up fighting the dude for my little potna.

Another time one of my other potnas had words with a dude from another city. He called my potna a bitch. Those are quick fighting words in prison. The other dude had a couple potnas with him and I was with my potna. We were on the yard at night and dude and my potna started fighting. My potna was getting the best of him but I still jumped in and helped my potna beat dude up. Dude's potna jumped in it and we had a little melee on the yard. I was the only one who got caught though. I got a write up for that and almost went to the hole.

This one time I just couldn't avoid this one issue from sending me to the hole. It involved the dude that shot me. I found out that he was on the other yard where I was at. He was spreading false rumors about me around on the yard. I sneaked over to his yard and made it to his building. He didn't even see me coming up on him. All he heard was me ask was he spreading rumors about me. I commenced to going up side his head and hitting him with everything I had. It wasn't long before the CO's came and pulled me off of him. They sent me to the hole and sent me to New Folsom, level four.

I went there because I am in the Triple CMS program. That's a program for the mentally ill. I went there and calmed down enough to get my points back down after a year.

From there I went to CMC state prison level three where I successfully got my points down too.

From there I came to San Quentin. Since being here at San Quentin I have been keeping a good program. I surround myself with positive people and stay out of trouble. Even though it's hard to stay out of all these people way because this prison is overcrowded, I still try.

EAST OAKLAND TIMES

The East Oakland Times, LLC (EOT) is a multi-media publication based in the San Francisco Bay Area. Founded by chief editor, Tio MacDonald, EOT has at its core three principles: the principle of the dignity of life, the principle of liberty, and the principle of tolerance. EOT supports the flourishing of civilization through the peace found by honoring these three stated principles.

Please remember by leaving a review you encourage others to buy the books in the My Crime series and thereby YOU support EOT's mission.

For exciting My Crime series bonus materials, such as audio interviews with the subjects of the My Crime series go to www.crimebios.com

Support the EOT by purchasing EOT produced e-books, print books, and audiobooks!

Be positive and stay blessed!
Do good! Love your neighbor and self!

Tio MacDonald
East Oakland Times
Chief Editor

EAST OAKLAND

www.ingramcontent.com/pod-product-compliance
Lightning Source LLC
Chambersburg PA
CBHW050556280326
41933CB00011B/1871